Jellyfish

by Martha E. H. Rustad

Consulting Editor: Gail Saunders-Smith, Ph.D.

Consultant: Jody Rake, Science Writer,
SeaWorld Education Department

Pebble Books

an imprint of Capstone Press
Mankato, Minnesota

Pebble Books are published by Capstone Press
151 Good Counsel Drive, P.O. Box 669, Mankato, Minnesota 56002
http://www.capstone-press.com

1 2 3 4 5 6 08 07 06 05 04 03

Library of Congress Cataloging-in-Publication Data
Rustad, Martha E. H. (Martha Elizabeth Hillman), 1975–
Jellyfish/by Martha E. H. Rustad.
p. cm.—(Ocean life)
Summary: Simple text and photographs describe the physical characteristics
and behavior of jellyfish.
Includes bibliographical references (p. 23) and index.
ISBN 0-7368-1656-9 (hardcover)
1. Jellyfishes—Juvenile literature. [1. Jellyfishes.] I. Title. II. Series.
QL377.S4 R87 2003
593.5′3—dc21   2002014774

Note to Parents and Teachers

The Ocean Life series supports national science standards for units on the diversity and unity of life. The series shows that animals have features that help them live in different environments. This book illustrates jellyfish and describes how they live. The photographs support early readers in understanding the text. The repetition of words and phrases helps early readers learn new words. This book also introduces early readers to subject-specific vocabulary words, which are defined in the Words to Know section. Early readers may need assistance to read some words and to use the Table of Contents, Words to Know, Read More, Internet Sites, and Index/Word List sections of the book.

Table of Contents

4

Jellyfish are
ocean animals.

6

Jellyfish can be many colors. Some jellyfish are clear.

Some jellyfish are small.
Some jellyfish are large.

Most jellyfish float slowly.
Jellyfish sometimes swim
quickly.

body

Jellyfish have a soft body shaped like a bell.

tentacles

14

Jellyfish have
many tentacles.

16

Jellyfish sting prey
with their tentacles.

18

Jellyfish move prey
into their mouth.

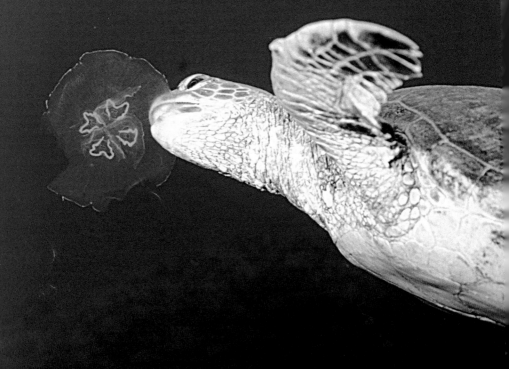

Predators sometimes
eat jellyfish.

Words to Know

float—to move slowly through water or air; most jellyfish float through the ocean.

mouth—a body part used to take in food

predator—an animal that hunts and eats other animals; jellyfish predators include sunfish, sea turtles, slugs, and other jellyfish.

prey—an animal that is hunted and eaten; jellyfish prey includes small ocean animals such as fish and krill.

sting—to hurt with a venomous tip; jellyfish tentacles have small, sharp, stinging cells.

swim—to move through water; jellyfish swim by sucking water into their bodies and pushing it out.

tentacle—a long, flexible arm of an animal; jellyfish sting prey with their tentacles.

Read More

George, Twig C. *Jellies: The Life of Jellyfish.*
Brookfield, Conn.: Millbrook Press, 2000.

Schaefer, Lola M. *Jellyfish.* Ooey-Gooey Animals.
Chicago: Heinemann Library, 2002.

Sharth, Sharon. *Jellyfish.* Naturebooks. Chanhassen,
Minn.: Child's World, 2001.

Internet Sites

Track down many sites about jellyfish.
Visit the FACT HOUND at *http://www.facthound.com*

IT IS EASY! IT IS FUN!

1) Go to *http://www.facthound.com*
2) Type in: 0736816569

3) Click on "FETCH IT" and FACT HOUND will find
   several links hand-picked by our editors.

Relax and let our pal FACT HOUND do the research
for you!

23

Index/Word List

Word Count: 58
Early-Intervention Level: 9

Credits

Steve Christensen, cover designer and illustrator; Patrick D. Dentinger,
    production designer; Kelly Garvin, photo researcher

Cole—V&W/Bruce Coleman Inc., 10
Digital Vision/Stephen Frink, 4
Eda Rogers, 1, 6
Fred Bavendam/Minden Pictures, 14
Jeff Rotman, 8, 20
Paul Sutherland Photography/sutherlandstock.com, 16, 18
Tom & Therisa Stack/Tom Stack & Associates, cover
Wernher Krutein/Photovault, 12